Testimonies Through a Cracked Window

Hip-Hop Poetry by Rob Nieves

Dedication:

Thank you Jesus for this ability to put words together in my own way. This is for the lost and broken individuals out there. I did my best to articulate my experiences in a way that is relatable while being personal

Introduction:

Welcome everyone into the mind of an abnormally normal man. I've always reflected poetically. From freestyling in my head, coming up with silly lullabies with my kids, and when I needed to ease my mind. I wrote. I decided to record my madness and tell my story. I don't expect these poems to reach everyone – I just hope they reach the ones who need to read them. To everyone who supports my work and finds something meaningful in these masterpieces: Thank you.

Thank you's:

To my children, Marcos and Mia: Jesus saved my soul, but you two saved my life. To Rissa, thank you for always caring about me! Boogs, my day one sister from another mister! My therapist, MR, and Localo, you guys have supported this book since day one, appreciate y'all! Kenni, big bro, you already know! My soldiers in heaven that watch over me, love each and every one of y'all. Everyone and anyone who supported me at any point in my life. Even if we don't talk anymore, you had a purpose in my life and in some way was part of my story. Thank you for your part in my evolution into becoming the man I am today.

Prologue

This is a poem that I experimented with. It's unorthodox and doesn't fit with the story I am telling. However, my story is about the forgotten and misunderstood. Instead of excluding it, I created this prologue before the journey begins.

Into the Wind

I love you, even if the words never cross your ears,
I hold them dear, not to pressure you into fear,
but as the warmth left behind when I am no longer near,
I send it into the wind, without seeking a return,
let it be your relief so it no longer burns,
may it brush your skin in the quietest moment,
a breeze so soft - it's gone before you know it.

ARCH IV — Judgment

Pivot 4 Wish upon a Star

ARCH V — SMOKE & LONGING

Pivot 5 Smoking on the Rooftop 4

ARCH VI — 4 THE CULTURE

Pivot 6 Different Type of Grass

ARCH VII — BECOMING

INTERLUDE Single Mothers

ARCH VIII — DUTY

Paying homage: Rose That Grew from Concrete 2025

ARCH IX — LETTERS

ARCH 1 — CRACKED

Buckle up, get out the strap, and get ready for a ride. I would try to tell you but honestly. I couldn't explain it. Let's go in 3...2...1

I Couldn't Explain It

I couldn't explain it, I just think differently.
Head full of evil thoughts, yet I speak spiritually.
I couldn't explain it - to you, it's more about what you see
Makes it easier to judge, plus ignore, what's good in me.

I couldn't explain it, I choose to politic in silence,
Trying to maintain peace. I'm quite familiar with violence.
I couldn't explain it, I can find the calm in the chaos
We live it, I mean, what dafuq could they say to us?

I couldn't explain it, I separate the weak and the obsolete.
Feel like a lone wolf, trapped in with a bunch of sheep.
I couldn't explain it - either way - you wouldn't listen.
Luckily for you, failure is an opportunity to gain wisdom.

I already explained it…is it my fault you couldn't get it?
Imagine if you took time to open your mind, think…nah, forget it.

Nurse! Nurse! Does anyone know CPR???

<u>Dead Inside</u>

Can't describe these demons inside of me.
What is presented is the outer side of me.
That misleads when you see a smiling me.
Because who I am really, died internally.

Tired of the facade, tired of wearing this mask.
Can I live - is the only thing that I ask.
I just want to find peace within myself.
God, please - I need You, I need Your help.

Can someone turn the light on? It's getting dark out here...

<u>untitled</u>

If truth be told, I can't say I desire to see my death.
When in actuality, I wish I failed to take a breath.
No comprehension for the ache that is defined as depressed.
I wasn't permitted to feel anything, because it produced my parents' stress.

Came of age, now I fail to regulate my emotions - I'm a wreck.
From my side of things, the only hope I have - is hopeless.
I am not notable - that's what my existence has determined to me.
Loathe that I'm puny - otherwise I'd pull the trigger, ending this cruelty.

Alright, you ready to see? I warned ya

<u>Mask off</u>

I am nothing but astray, ruptured and a miswired soul.
Shoehorning fragments, been doing so since 7 years old.
My only compass had no direction, no map for the road.
So I chose the darkest alley I could find to carry my load.

Burnt, beat, shot, bruised - that's just physically.
Conditioned to believe I couldn't add up statistically.
Some days I say, "Lord can we skip to the end of the script?"
If You close the chapter early, remember that I didn't quit.

I see my kids and wish I had something better to offer.
Praying my failures won't deter their chance to prosper.
I'm the mirror for my kin, they won't see no parts of me.
I'd have better luck losing a buck, than winning the lottery.

This isn't paranoia- it's patterned in my fucked up imagination.
Hope? That checked out, left me waiting at the train station.
Stay away from me, I'm corroded and will take you under.
Ah, what the fuck, you're toxic too, hey here's my number.

I want to try - actually who the hell am I fucking kidding?
Besides, I'm closer to the end than I ever was to the beginning.

If you relate to this. None of it was your fault, ok.

Shame

Ever walked inside a room, then told to close the door?
Knowing you're gonna do something you don't want to anymore.
At first it appeared fun, for it was introduced as a game.
Except the only reward gained was soreness and pain.

Confused about myself, for other men do not excite me.
I like girls - am I supposed to? At this age, they don't like me...
It doesn't help my confidence much that I'm obese and ugly.
So I pretend it's one of them when the men start to touch me.

Shame and guilt haunt my thoughts - I want to tell an adult.
Because of fear, I didn't fight back. Will they say it's my fault?
I doubt they would even believe me - tell me to shut the fuck up.
Still young, still small, too weak - unfortunately, at this point I'm stuck.

Eventually I got older, got bolder, and now it's finally over.
I found a coping mechanism - as a teen, I was rarely caught sober.
Decades have passed, and I'd like to say I no longer have shame.
I do.
I know I shouldn't, but I ponder: what if...I just said no to their game?

The hardest part about being yourself is, people get to know you...

<u>Vulnerability</u>

Vulnerability? That was a luxury from where I come from.
Any sign of being soft, automatic target to get jumped on.
Cracking underneath, heart pulsating, pumping in my neck.
I chug along - no indication nor do I even look stressed.

Alone is when I implode - how much can one suppress?
Shit hurts - body twinges and is faltering from all the distress.
Thoughts persistently running - so much so, it feels unsettled when it's not.
I'd tell you what I ponder - unfortunately, most of that shit I forgot.

I wail in my pillow - some nights I feel this wetness all over my cheeks.
Tell myself I'm fierce so I believe, even in the components I know are weak.
OK, get it together - snap back to reality.
Solidity is all I know to obstruct my mortality.

So back outside I go - what's within, no one may ever know.
Steadfastly mounted to the tenth toe - and stoicism is all I'll ever show.

Man, sometimes I really wish I could shut the fuck up.

Prisoner in my Own Mind

Sprawled in bed, I toss and turn, my mind is constantly churning.
It's 2 in the morning, thoughts are roaring - you'd think it'd be concerning.
I replay the day, I can't escape - when will this shit be over.
Finally reach for my blunt, light it up - I cannot do life sober.

It's what if this and what if that, what if I shut the fuck up - shit!
Too many thoughts, I don't know what problems actually exist.
Even make arguments with myself - time for the looney bin.
Tired of losing sleep over some shit that didn't even happen.

Alright, get it together - this is a war between me, myself, and I.
Obviously I can't run, so instead I suppress it and hide.
This is what I mean when I say I'm a prisoner in my own mind.
Except there's no EOS, I'm stuck in this loop until the end of time.

I want to accept what I can't control, I don't know if I'll succeed.
I know what's in myself, and that's what makes it hard to believe.
Only if all of the world's problems could be solved with a bag of weed.
Ah, who am I bullshitting - I want that so I can finally fall back asleep.

*EOS - end of sentence....if you don't know what that means....you don't know what that means.

Should I start looking forward to something, I've been asking myself that in life...

<u>untitled Pt. 2</u>

There's an agony in my soul, that I know the reality.
Far differentiates the desire I have in me.
It's ok to hurt - the pain is natural.
Raise your eyes to God - He got you.

Actions speak louder than words used against me.
It's when I act out of emotion they try to fence me.
In any case, I'll be myself - because that's who I are.
Honestly, they always cheer for me - but from afar.

No point to anguish - I know I'm a star.
Radiate brightly - I'ma raise that bar.

Pivot | Smoking on the Rooftop |

Smoking on the Rooftop

Sitting, blunt in my hand, 'bout to light that bitch up.
Living this thing called life, and man, that bitch rough.
Let the fire hit the blunt, take a puff, now lean back.
Exhale all the bullshit - send it off, I don't retract.

All alone, in the zone, staring at the sky.
Illmatic - Life's a bitch and then you die.
I concur with Az, that's why I puff lye.
Struggles will always arise, but for now I'm high.....goodbye.

ARCH II — GOD & GRACE

Some shit gotta change, it be feeling like something missing. Ever felt like that?

Is This the End

If I could end it all - oh, that would be nice.
End the misery - oh yes, what a delight.
The pressure is too much - never ending.
Tired of putting up a smile, tired of pretending.

The show is over, folks - time for the fireworks.
Oh boo hoo, stop crying, bitch - what you tired for?
Things aren't going your way - is life just too hard?
Instead of the Ruger, how about you turn to God?

He already died for you - dafuq else you want him to do?
Put your faith in Him - He has nothing to prove.
Let go of what you can't control - let God set you on His path for you today.
It was always there, fool - open your eyes and get out of your own way.

Even when I am alone, I know I am truly not.

God's with me

Thought I was broken till God showed me that I am unbreakable.
It took me a minute to see it, so I guess I learned about patience too.
Succumbing to the anguish, looking at myself, I faced the truth.
Refocused - except on the haters, for they can do what haters do.

Never perfect, but perfection is perfected through reflection and acceptance.
I started on my knees, confessed to God, and requested repentance.
With each tear I felt my burdens fall - that's how I knew that God didn't forsake me.
Don't mistake me, I have stumbled lately, but before I fall - I know God will save me.

God, please give me a recent example to explain to these folks.

<u>God I need help</u>

God, I need help - I acknowledge without You I am defenseless.
My faith is strong to take on what the enemy sends us.
So here's my situation:
I trust in Jesus to get me through what I am facin'.

Took a look at my finances and got to matchin'.
Getting worried - instead of addin', shit felt like subtraction.
Realized I couldn't afford to keep my crib on my own.
Stuck having to rent a room, but I'm not alone.

I got two kids that I split custody with they mom.
Mention them and folks ain't let me say what's goin' on.
Weeks go by, and finally I found a place to live.
The lady tell me even fathers deserve their kids.

Then she tells me she'll get back at me in a few.
Hours later she returned with bad news - shoulda knew.
Long story short - I didn't get the room.
First thing I did was look up to God and said, "I have faith in You."

Watcha know - hours later my phone rings out the blue.
It's another family giving me an interview.
Mentally I was through, so I was straight up and spoke the truth.
The man said, "Sounds like you could use a blessin' dude."

That's why I trusted You, Jesus, through what I was facin'.
I knew He wouldn't leave alone through my situation.
My faith remains strong to take on what the enemy sends us.
When I have God's help, I am never defenseless.

Fuck, decisions, decisions. But damn, something's gotta give!

The Choice

Nothing like lying in a cell pulling a wedgie out your county blues.
Salivating about smoking bud with orange hairs and a purple hue.
Snap out and back to stinky dudes taking a shit in plain view.
Questioning the decisions I made, and about the life I choose.

Leaning back, I reach under my pillow and grab my Bible.
John 8:7, I have no idea why, but that verse is so vital.
I never really accepted it, I just went to church my whole life.
I guess I never understood what it meant to choose Christ.

I say my prayers, go to chapel, read my chapters…still feel the same.
Not expecting a magician, but listen, can something for the better change?
Then one day in the shower, I couldn't take it anymore, I chose to let go.
Tears crashing down my face, plus the shower - a moment so spiritual.

A shiver trickled down my back as I sensed my soul cleanse.
I confessed my darkest moments, then asked God to pardon my sins.
I looked up, water now in my mouth as I continue to speak to Him.
Jesus, if you'll have me, I choose you - please show me how to begin.

It's not easy trusting something that is not tangible. Once you do....

Faith

Again I wake up to these four walls but nothing's the same.
Keeping quiet because of shame, never dare I complain.
When you do, nothing matters nor will it bring any change.
Additionally, now you've revealed what nerves your pain.

What's insane is the claim that pain indicates you're alive.
Sure blood flows in the veins, smiles appear as pride.
Shit might as well be formaldehyde that won't let your tissues die.
I could imagine it's the reason I have no maggots growing inside.

No more energy for others needing me to fix their situation.
My quarrels are met with me standing alone when I face em'.
Not that I need anyone assisting with my own complications.
I have God's plan to fulfill, hardest challenge is maintaining patience.

There's a long trip ahead of me as I limber down this unsteady road.
This was not my chosen route, but the one God allowed me to go.
They say good things come to those who are able to wait.
I say, good things come to those who move forward in faith.

Pivot 2 smoking on the Rooftop 2

Smoking on the Rooftop 2

As I continue to cherish this gift called aging, inhaling this orange loud.
Taking this moment to exhale all the emotions, storage in the cloud.
This is my escape, I don't bother anyone or make scenes.
Peace is all I care for and I'll protect it by any means.

So I sit up high on the roof and kick it back.
Music penetrating the drums, mind's starting to relax.
Watch the sun slip and fall down past the horizon.
Oh my bad, don't mind me....I'm just high, man.

ARCH III — THE STREETS MADE ME

Wanna take a pit stop with me? Wipe your feet please, this is my home!

Summerset

Summerset, a place where niggas will beat you and take your shit.

Keep the four fifth gripped, strip you from the neck to your bracelet.

Back when cars could be jimmied, we'd pop the lock and take all they got.

Too small to drive the whip, we walked our asses down to the pawn shop.

Puerto Ricans, Blacks with our boombox screaming out Hip-Hop.

We just chillin' minding our business - here come the cops.

Throw us face first to the ground, lying motionless, still yelling at us to stop.

Not known for good decisions - still smart enough not to get caught.

I learned no door is locked - learned that mixture to cook rock.

Also, how to drip, take no shit, comport as a man, and run the block.

There's a code, but when shit hits the fan, most don't follow.

It's too late by the time you discover that your man is hollow.

The girls around already damaged, freeing up the goods.

That's why we learn to not love, just fuck bitches in the hood.

This is where I'm from, and I loved it, no reason to lie about it.

Just a Spic Nigga, aka a product of my environment.

Just because you saw my home, doesn't mean u kno me.

<u>u don kno me</u>

Keep a chrome magnum 'cause you never know what's gon' happen.
Be when you mindin' yo bidness, they wanna force a reaction.
I'm a good person in an environment where you can't show it.
See a weakness, and it'll be used against you before ya know it.

So when I stand 10 toes down and I look stoic,
I got a .357 on my side, and I'm not afraid to blow it.
It's not where my mind's at, but again, you wanna cause friction.
Your choice, but you might wanna pause before you cause a confliction.

Again, I'm a good person - so be careful what you show me.
I'll match yo energy, homie - remember, u don know me.

Not every street nigga a gangsta, some of us build teams of our own.

Not a gangsta

Through the perspective of a lens found neglected,
Still overcame the false narrative that I once accepted.
Yes, the normality of violence mixed with manipulated deception
Could trap an impressionable individual who'll shoulder any form of attention.

Now, I respected the group that ran a whole section,
Pursued my own passion, regarded the line, and never stepped in.
Had a few escapades that had concluded in violence –
Like Fight Club, we don't talk about it – radio silence.

Peace shall always be the immediate option,
In spite of survival instincts learned but never forgotten.

Ever seen a rose grow out of concrete? Yes, no, maybe???

<u>Don't Bury Me a G</u>

If I die tonight, don't bury me a G,
bury me a nigga that rose out the concrete,
took my dreams from fantasy and made them my reality,
transformed triumphs that originated from tragedies.

You see, the odds can't define me, therefore I'm unique.
I've never experienced luxury, I resided in the streets.
If you catch up to me, you'd still never get to me.
You can't fuck with me - riches don't mean shit to me.

You can get stuck quick - I sell it back to you.
Done it before - don't make me react to you.
I'm humble, and I stick to my business.
It takes a lot before I'm like, "Who the fuck is this?"

Look up to the Almighty and already ask for forgiveness.
I remind myself - a wrong move can turn into a sentence.

Why is it the only time I feel unsafe is not when the guns are around, not when there's drugs and half stripped people passed out in awkward positions. Nah, whenever the fucking police be around is when I fear for my life and safety.

<u>Fuck Tha Police</u>

usually I keep my anger controlled, but for 12 I'ma let it go!
Fuck it, why not - I'll give them the same respect that they show.
I'm human, fool - I bleed red, and I need oxygen to breathe too.
Tell the truth, there's a significant difference between me and you.

No, it's not the amount of melanin I possess in my skinsuit.
It's that I'm not a pussy - I control my fear and have intent when I shoot.
The laws were made against us, not in order to protect us.
No need to correct us - we're the only ones to resurrect us.

You've done enough to show how you continuously disrespect us.
The claim of fear is just your pathetic excuse to be reckless.
Even when it's done peacefully, you get upset when we protest.
But - when we took a knee, it wasn't to choke someone to death.

I may be an asshole, but you can't call me a liar.

Why lie

Man, I ain't got time for the bullshit.
What for what - man, lies don't prove shit.
Contrary - truth got the power to move shit.
Open one's eyes to how ya ain't never do shit.

Me? I don't have that type of problem.
My actions are what speaks to how I resolve 'em.
Integrity is the main ingredient to my ethical recipe.
Honesty is simply the basis of my pedigree.

How can you expect to be respected when you're known a deceiver?
Or even be trusted because you mislead with a calm demeanor.
If I hurt your feelings, sorry - but I'm not gon' be apologetic.
You may not like what I said, but I hope you don't forget it.

Truth shows flaws - now the opportunity is presented.
The opportunity to attack those same flaws and shed it.
You'll wanna thank me later, but I won't be around to accept it.
If I said something that made you feel that I care, I hope you don't forget it.

I don't say shit just to say shit - which means I meant it.
I got a big heart, but that bitch done got shredded.
Too many pieces to make a valid effort to recover.
So I move forward, one foot in front of the other.

Though speaking the truth may have me finding myself alone,
I have peace - a journey most aren't destined to find on their own.

Pay attention, stakes are getting high!

Play to win

Encounters within the inhumane darkness of this nation.
It'd be an act of deceit if I didn't admit participation.
Fully locked in, can't take my sight off the opposition.
Standing by my word, live by my desired proposition.

I'm confident, but also honest with myself, I know my limits.
Keep my eyes on the prize, refraining from ignorant gimmicks.
You see, in this game it's about who's the last one to finish.
Most take a trip up the river if they don't sleep with the fishes.

It could be the same niggas who had you over for family dinners,
Plotting their own succession, excluding you from the pictures.
That's why I kept watch on my 6, my 3, and my 9.
While I packed a .38 in my boot, with fifteen in my nine.

If I fell, the correlation's directly the result of unpreparedness.
The idea is to wither old using wisdom and maintain awareness.
Accepting defeat is an event I never take into consideration.
I plan for victory: include the glory, minus the reservations.

Sometimes you go out minding your business, sometimes business finds you.

<u>Dec. 11</u>

It was a chill night, a recent cold front's residue.
Warm enough to take a late night trip with the crew.
Hit a red light, I wasn't feeling the look on the next dude.
Looked at him straight up, asked, "The fuck wrong with you?"

His manhood got tested, so he pulled out his baby .22.
I laughed and said, "Nigga, you tryna tickle me, fool?"
Shoulda seen his face drop - motherfucker looked confused.
Green light hit, the car split, a few seconds later...BOOM!

Started driving...then my right leg started going numb - is this anxiety?
Everyone checked except me - I could tell if something took flight in me.
I gave in, looked - oh shit, I got hit, right on my calf.
Everyone freaked out except me - I just laughed.

Nurses were busy, I stepped outside to smoke a weed-filled cigarette.
Hospital patched me up - told the cops I ain't know shit.
When I described the shooter, it was someone my boy recognized.
I won't say no more - because if there is one thing, I tell no lies.

Pivot 3 Wish upon a star

Wish upon a star

Oh shit, look at what occurred when I lifted my eyes high.
Observed a moving object, it's a star that fell from the sky.
I heard a saying that in this moment to make a wish.
Render a deep breath as I put some thought into this.

Actually, not really because it's evident, as to who benefits.
Not for me, but I ask for long-term happiness for my kids.
Success if I get two wishes, more than anything I want them content.
As a father and man of God, I gotta protect what was heaven-sent.

ARCH IV — Judgment

Some people are quick to judge, but is your house in order?

In the Eyes of America

I was born in a country, already destined to lose.
Portrayed as ignorant, supposedly missing some tools.
Capable of speaking a 2nd language? Nah, that ain't cool.
Oh, got a little accent? Instantly perceived as a fool.

Silently I watch with quiet confidence, intellectually profound.
Actions reveal far more, it's easy to discard your sound.
If your perception of me is poor...sorry how's that my problem?
What you ignore can still grow, to a point you can't solve them.

There is nothing to solve, I'm a human, nothing is new.
Your lack of discernment, is not my burden to carry through.
I could never shit on the faces, of those who paved me a way.
Many wished to be here, they are no longer in existence today.

It's the price we pay for freedom, it's a costly affair.
Still we show pride, you can feel it on the scars I bare.
Somewhere says all men are created equal, if that's to be true.
Maybe the person you're to take a deep look at is...well...it's you..

Once a man, always my Abuela's baby.

En los Ojos de Mi Abuela

In the eyes of my grandma, I am a child who could do no wrong.
The legacy of her deceased daughter, carried by her son.
She didn't realize the horrors I faced and had to process.
No matter what, she saw innocence beneath the lostness.

I did my best to make her proud, but the perils of life took their grasp.
Her vision for me versus my reality were engaged in war, creating contrast.
I could never live up to her expectations, my experiences teeming with violence.
Before my dreams could become wet, I consequently feared closing my eyelids.

In her eyes I was not the problem - it's that I "chose" bad apples.
Yet I'm the one people choose when a problem needs to be tackled.
Internally I crumbled, not because of the judge, Abuela's eyes saw me in shackles.
Only she showed up while I faced consequences for doing what I had to.

I turned myself around, stopped crying just because I was a victim.
understood my choices were mine, and stopped blaming the system.
En los ojos de mi Abuela, I will always be this baby boy.
I love you, mi Abuela, but that version of me was destroyed.

Bendición Abuela, R.I.P. and thank you for not losing sight of the good in me.

My turn....

<u>Who I Am</u>

I'm an attested soldier who never chose to enter myself into battle.
Still rose to a master chief in the streets, protecting my own castle.
I know my own soul and the fact I am powered by a good heart.
Despite my family, society, and 12's attempts to pull it apart.

My hands remain filthy, too much foreign DNA in my pores.
Who I was when I had to be him - is not who I am anymore.
The pain I learned to numb backfired, it became my superpower.
Now I stay clean but that does not mean, I forgot how to shower.

Once upon I cowered, now I stand tall amongst the crowd.
Never do I seek attention, it's my aura that astounds.
Yes, I have guilt, but it is no longer something I choose to carry.
The heaviness has spilt, building towards a life that is merry.

Now I have children, so a new legacy by me...is to be established.
I didn't know mine, but rest assured they will know who their dad is.
If I ever loved you, know that it was real, for that I can't fake.
Apologies to those I hurt, I ask for forgiveness....if it's not too late.

Pivot 4 smoking on the Rooftop 3

Smoking on the Rooftop 3

What a perfect night, everything except these fucking mosquitoes.
The other night I saw a star drop, made a wish for my kids though.
I'm good....shit, long as I stay getting supplied with this indo.
So much more freeing outside, better than looking through the window.

I needed a moment like this, long days stretch into the night.
Light the end of my Dutch and take a puff as I take flight.
This is my time to unfold and make my own personal amends.
Like Styles said, I light a blunt because never will the struggle end.

ARCH V — SMOKE & LONGING

What, I'm not heartless, I'm actually empathetic...yes I am.

Thinking of you

Sometimes I can't focus, because I'm too busy thinking about you.
Not sure what is better, fighting for us pushed you out of view.
Days turned into weeks, questions without answers, what do I do.
The longing hasn't softened, is this normal or am I just a fool.

You would tell me it's not that I care, it's that I got used to you.
Yea I'm smashing chicks, you know that I'd still choose you.
Not like I need you, I'm doing fine, don't want to confuse you.
Kids are good, work is great, really right now life is beautiful.

It's more of, if I feel this strong after knowing what went wrong.
It's stupid to let what we have die and just carry on.
I want to send a message, just not quite sure I know what to say.
Probably keep it simple, ask her to tell me something random about her day.

Eventually I know I will, when I am ready to do it my way.
Wondering if you know that I still think of you almost everyday.

Is this shit really real?

What's Love?

Is love just an emotion, or something you can feel - like a breeze off the ocean?
Maybe it's a drug, because the way people change...it gotta be potent.
Why does it tend to feel great - then rip the air out your lungs as you suffocate?
The truth seems to be fake, constantly confused -
and that be the shit I hate.

Have you ever wondered if you found the one, just a bit too late?
Realizing this life you live isn't fate - just the one you needed to create.
Now you drift over to an alternative state, start daydreaming to liberate.
Why with love you couldn't wait? Yet with everything else you hesitate...

Not everyone you meet is a mistake, but it doesn't mean they're the one either.

Affinity

I was at my lowest of lows, and you were there for me.
Humiliated by my circumstance - you didn't care, you just cared for me.
Couldn't render a thing - neither did you ever require or even ask from me.
Complacent with the bare necessities to establish memories you have from me.

Mutually supported one another - always 100, never went half on me.
Defying the odds because you didn't desert me like my past homies.
I know you I owe you zip, nada - but anything you want, you will have of me.
When you desire distance, embrace your solitude - you know where I'm at, shawty.

We were once inextricable, but now we proceed independently down our own paths.
Knowing every time they cross, we integrate and coalesce - manifesting into more laughs.

Eh, you might want to close your eyes when you read this one.

Intrinsic Enchantment

I'm hesitant to comprehend, but something about you is dissimilar.
Attention has been obtained - the uncertainty is superior to the familiar.
Honestly, I'd dispense an hour or two citing all the qualities I appreciate.
Intellectual, wondrous - spicy enough to whisper intentions to penetrate.

Might be a good girl, but I fucked you like a thotty.
Multitude of orgasms prior to my ejaculation in your body.
An enchantment so intrinsic that it lasted longer than intended.
No reason to differentiate a good time - this too has ended.

Is it just me, or everyone at least got that one ex they can call to go out and play? Really, just me??

<u>Ghetto Love</u>

It's kind of odd how two people can be so deeply compounded in connection.
No wedding bells or hands held, its strength doesn't rely on attention.
They go their separate ways, with one hand still gripped to a tether.
They'll never be, officially, but will always find ways to be together.

It may sound weird, but it's a bond that's cultivated in toxic behavior.
Designed to be easy and fun, yet always ends up in failure.
They fantasized about past lives where their matrimony was secured.
For this life is too difficult to maintain, after all their mutilated hearts endured.

She dreams of aging towards mortality and living free in a foreign land.
When those plans are recited, it's with me by her side, not her man.
See, there are too many distractions, you can see them steadily juggle.
They just want peace from the hustle, a future foreseen without struggle.

Neither can give what the other truly deserves, well...not sustainably.
So they check in, give updates about the kids, and fornicate shamelessly.
Honestly, it could all just end at any given moment if one just cuts the cord.
Neither will, because the cost from the loss is something either can't afford.

Things change, just the way life is.

Sorry That I Hurt You

I smoke and trace the sparks that caused our friction.
Confused by my own contradictions.
Through it all, I still hold one conviction.
We go together - I can't see a different vision.

I heard you - now I see why you said I don't listen.
Time apart has brought clarity - can I be forgiven?
Dragging chains of could've-beens and questionable decisions.
I just wanted you to smile - not cause any tension.

Ever step out of your norm and find something, you think it's going well and then.....

Wasted Love

In a season of self-rehabilitation - in other words, I was doing me.
Minding my own business, yet she slipped in fluidly.
Started with questions, only due to my profession,
Then the progression of her follow-up sessions.

Congruently, flirtation forged us into conversations.
Holistic mutual respect evolved into intimate relations.
A perfect soul carrying burdens not of her own.
It took its toll, and the cracks became visibly shown.

Never released judgement - shit, I too have my issues.
Never concerned for perfection - I just fucking dig you.
The water crested too high; I knew emotionally you were drowning.
Not a reflection of our connection, but a victim to your surroundings.

Then it began - the push started matching the pull.
Self-respect didn't allow for indecision; and she was no fool.
The unfortunate result was her doing what she had to do.
As so was mine - watching her through the window as she flew.

You might want to close your eyes reading this again, one more time...

Intrinsic Enchantment 2

I find this intriguing - because typically, she's not my style.
Still, I shot my shot to dominate and make her howl.
Started with a kiss, then licked her all the way down.
Spawning bliss as her trembles vibrate through the ground.

At the moment of climax, her scream is so profound.
Now I enter the castle - like a king taking his crown.
The physical nature intensifies boiling in the moment.
up until the pressure releases inside her, emptying my scrotum.

Pleasurable and rambunctious - but fuck it we know it's temporary.
Shit 'bout as real as the 30th of February.
Even if we tried, we know eventually I'll fail.
We're both broken, this ain't no new fairytale.

If I'm the smoke then you're the fire that set off the alarm.
Time to wake up before either of us do any harm.
There's no reason to make it more than what it is.
Even if you never find another me - we'll still live.

Sounds like it might be time to take a walk.

Go Along Your Way

When I try to save the connection we had, it's not that I don't get it.
It's that I know what we had was real and I don't want to regret it,
I spoke out of my heart; though, I know, this can't be saved by reasoning.
But your decision has been made and I find it bewildering.

How does something that was once on fire instantly turn brick?
Couldn't get enough of me and now you don't give a shit.
We both know you do - that's why you still pop up to check on me.
I respond, but each and every time I care less, respectfully.

Avoid your feelings - I guess that's how you feel safe.
I moved on by now; for some reason, I still show you grace.
Go ahead, take care, and do what you feel is best for you.
You got what you desired. I'm gone - only one left is you.

Pivot 5 Smoking on the Rooftop 4

Smoking on the Rooftop 4

Suddenly awoken, I stretch over, grab my clip and dipped outside.
This may sound familiar, but over the horizon's a new sunrise.
Call it what you want, that pink and purple got me mesmerized.
Been called it all by now, so there's nothing left of me to criticize.

Once I figured out how to focus forward, I learned to not look behind.
What you don't know won't hurt you, still I always keep a clever mind.
Always told the truth, especially when I had to tell a lie.
Why do you bother listening to me when you know I'm high?

ARCH VI — 4 THE CULTURE

I see you looking at me, looking at you...what's up?

I know u see me watchin

I see you over there watching me.
I'll stay here and sit back confidently.
See, I know what I bring to the table.
Not gon act desperate, n' go chase you.

Not saying I won't approach you.
Just I'll take my time before I encroach you.
Right when you think I ain't coming - here I go.
She over here laughing, relaxing - yeah, I know.

Decide to get up and make some traction.
You know what's next - if not, watch out for the back end.

Time to stunt real quick, not yo atypical poet...and you know it!

<u>Mic check (freestyle) Pt. 1</u>

I can respectfully be disrespectful.

Take from yo ass, simultaneously be helpful.

You can escape the fall, but you can't get on my level.

I'm God's child - yet down the block lies the devil.

If you're arrogant enough to challenge me, then go ahead n' step to this.

Best be prepared to cover more surface area than Los Angeles.

Hold my blunt - it'll only take me a sec to handle this.

Swear they the shit, when they just fuckin amateurs.

Thumping on my chest - I'm King Kong in this bitch.

Taking off so many heads, got labeled a terrorist.

A God-given talent that I learned I possess.

I can do anything - (How?) it's called confidence.

So indestructible, swear my ass gotta be conceited.

Look into my eyes, tell me you don't see it.

I'd keep going, but I'd turn this event into pay per view.

Yeah, I fucked your moms - so what, you gon hate her too?

(Sound of the mic dropping.....footsteps slowly fading away)

I can do this all day, but I'll just do one more!

Mic check (freestyle) Pt.2

All I ever needed was one shot, one opportunity.
Already mastered the art of authoring eulogies.
It's the fear of failure that indeed fuels me.
Transforms into lessons - that's what moves me.

Got a bachelor's in business while I mastered the Hard Knocks.
I can formulate a plan and show old marks from hot glocks.
Overlooked and unnoticed - definition of an underdog.
Don't care what anyone think - I know what I'm capable of.

My family failed me, America failed me - it's ok, I got me.
I understand that's all I, plus my kids, are ever gon' need.
I'm not mature - the world allowed me to grow wisely.
I heard the good die young - that's why y'all despise me.

Put so many in the dirt - I don't take my breaths lightly.
And for what it's worth, everyone's still alive inside me.
DNA of a giant, though I stand barely above 5 feet.
It's the fight in me that hits the jugular precisely.

If you can't understand me, then I'll accept that I am overstood.

Being Overstood

My complexity measures at a depth that can't be reached by destiny.
Even if you didn't understand it, you understood I said it excellently.
Between arrogance and confidence, I lean all the way towards confidently.
You could augment me all you want but I will not be used - not even sparingly.

Trust issues yea, but when it matters most I'm the only one to care for me.
Except that toxic ex that likes rough sex and if I slip, she put up that bail money.
You know it's funny what people do for love, I can give a fuck if you love me.
Let me cum and go to make c-notes while I raise my kids - only if I'm lucky.

My top don't drop but I got my face hanging out the window.
It's moments like these I feel so free as if I'm reaching my crescendo.
I wish upon whatever goes beyond, to maintain my soul's energy.
It's not my fault if you overstood, and got frustrated over my complexity.

If the sky is the limit, what are we doing about space?

Sky's the Limit

Momma said sky's the limit, so I aim for the galaxy.
Overcame the harsh reality of surviving casualties.
Even when I fell, the rise happened rapidly.
While your shit rose gradually, then you blamed it on gravity.

Nothing strapping me, with or without my sanity.
I'ma shine so bright, even the blind'll get mad at me.
I was born ready, not like anyone catchin' me.
Besides, niggas run once they realize my savagery.

No need to cheat, for me winning happens naturally.
R.I.P. Kobe, now I live on with that Mamba mentality.
Still remember back in the days they used to laugh at me.
I stayed climbing, stayed focused, nothing distracting me.

Actually, that's why factually, ain't nobody bad as me.
Shit's blasphemy; to think otherwise is a fucking fantasy.
My reality registers beyond the mental capacity.
The sky ain't my limit, it's my starting point. Stop asking me!

Pivot 6 Different Type of Grass

Different Type of Grass

Came up in the streets, now I'm raising kids in the burbs.
Glad I escaped the jungle, but there's benefits I observed.
Accustomed to the struggle, I perform at my peak under duress.
The hustle built muscle memory, now I'm getting legitimate checks.

If I don't got what I need, I'll make it... or figure it out off the cuff.
Don't understand the concept of broke, I've never had enough.
For my kids there's a gap - it's my job to provide what they lack.
Grateful for the benefits, but other than that, I'll never move back.

ARCH VII — BECOMING

Life has a funny way of having painful necessities.....

Letting Go

The most difficult option in life is one I've had to choose often.
Letting go of someone while knowing they'll never be forgotten.
Reasons can vary, but usually it's between dignity and peace.
Still an agonizing release - so distraught I fear my heart will cease.

Sometimes the shoe's on the other foot - meaning it's their choice.
The sting comes as a shock to my core, but I gotta stay poised.
Not all are meant to stay - as the clock ticks away, so does the sting.
Wish I could say they came back - truthfully, that is not a thing.

I remember laying around hopeless - but of course they can return.
I won't make it easy - my energy needs to be earned.
When I walked, I reminded myself who I am - then built myself up.
Transitioned into someone I can stare in the mirror and love.

I teared up because it hurts, but it's the act I needed to evolve.
The hardest reality was wishing to fix what has no resolve.
Respect starts from within - that was the exact moment I realized my worth.
I let go - not because the task is simple, but because I know what I deserve.

I need a minute, let me just float freely for a bit.

Auto Pilot

I cruise the streets, unaware of the despair that I bear.
Hand on the wheel, blowing out that good kush in the air.
Got my jams bumping, JL Audio W3s in the back thumping.
Not for nothing, I'm in the mood to get into something.

Handled that, now I'm back, feeling kinda hungry.
See Mofongo con carne frita, fuck it bro, take all my money.
It's not funny...actually it is, I don't know, but can I live?
Got some dutches, told my niggs meet me at my crib.

Numb to the world, you could say I stopped giving a shit.
I just move how I do, always find what I need to get.
In a world that functions off chaos, I'll just sit back and observe.
Set to autopilot, why fight it? All I want to do is smoke some herb.

Alright, I'm back and I'm in beastmode!

<u>Metamorphosis</u>

You may be aware of my experiences but lately.

Going through a metamorphosis that's changed me.

Who knew the weight of the rocks is all it took to train me.

To pick up the scattered pieces in order to re-arrange me.

Becoming the things I used to think that I can't be.

My doubters getting mad and so what, they already hate me.

Product of my environment makes a lot sense to why I'm so crazy.

I just say it as it is because I'm exactly as this world made me.

Ever get these urges you can't control? Like why am I short of breath, why is my heart pounding, why are my palms sweaty, just why?

Anxiety

Interpretations differ, but I ponder, "Truly what's anxiety?"
To me it's a voice that runs thoughts constantly inside of me.
Perspiring through my pores, even sense a drip on my balls.
Take a stand, and collapse as my blood pressure suddenly falls.

My fear of the miscalculation from others - keeps my heart racin'.
How that need to know the answer NOW - makes me impatient.
I mean well internally, but everything I say comes out different.
Then nervousness kicks in - I'm caged in a mentally muddled prison.

Yet on the exterior - the appearance is composed and gathered.
Heartache, regrettable decisions, let-downs from what mattered.
Unsure how much is on me - but it seems like that's my pattern.
It'd be nice to leave the chaos - rise up from the shit I sat in.

Peace is far-fetched, yet sincerely it is my passion.
The outcome is uncertain but I know what needs to happen.
The weight is too heavy, however, I dig deep and use every fiber.
Take a deep breath in...then out...a reminder...I'm a mu'fucking survivor.

Alright, let's pause for a moment.

Restraint

Gotta shut off and find restraint.
Regardless, I have to tell myself no - I can't.
It's confusing - not gon' lie it throws me off.
Sitting in the dark, getting intoxicated on the porch.

What do you do when you can't control a situation?
Me? I treat it like fear and just face it.
Focus on what's in front of me.
Can't let my emotions fuck with me.

I got kids, and they share the love with me.
Not their burden to see how fear and pain is touching me.
I'm torn at the seams, dragging myself to the finish line.
God on my side - but damn, yo...fuck this grind.

How strong does God expect me to be?
it's like I'm blind, and He still expects me to see.
Then I remember - that's why it's called faith,
it's the Lord giving me the ability to have restraint.

Not gon clean out the closet, but I am going to release and move on.

Mi Familia

They tried to outcast me, exile me from the family.
Pause - walking away is a gesture I'd perform happily.
I comprehend your denial of what happened to me.
Ignorance, however, does not erase reality.

Resilience is my character; I don't give a fuck is my mentality.
I did not change overnight, the transition happened gradually.
Got met with distance, after all I wanted was accountability.
Why face yourself, when it's easier to get rid of me.

Now a maverick, blossoming over those that abandoned me.
Peace exposed in solitude - and I mean that candidly.
Finally I can exhale, no more tragedy upon tragedy.
A free bird, floating in the wind despite gravity.

God, weed, and my seeds are all I require.
Truth is a bitch, but I could never be a liar.
I detached from you - but on God, I wish mi familia the best.
This is what you wanted.....So to y'all, I cease to exist.

The hard part is done, time to stand on business.

No Looking Back

Pain - it's the reason why you stop, chest tightens, breath caught.
Hesitation...procrastination...now you rather not.
Shame sets in because you know you should be tough.
See, pain is also mental, as if the physical wasn't enough.

Concluding certain outcomes that actually don't exist,
conflicting battles inside the shadows beneath the surface.
Can't ensure any alternatives, yet I can say this:
suck it up buttercup - you have to take risks.

When fear becomes triumphant, the cost is too expensive.
The tolls add up, rendering the fall to be relentless.
Regulate your composure, take a deep breath.
Look ahead, gather forward - congrats on your first step.

Withdraw from reversing - doubtfulness is a set of traps.
You made it this far...trust me when I say, fuck a relapse.

I might have a chip on my shoulder, just a tiny ity bity one.

The underdog

Overlooked, miscalculated, and let's add undervalued.
Always critiqued by someone that knows nothing about you.
Never given a chance, yet they found reasons to doubt you.
What isn't realized is silent determination cultivating a stout you.

Fuck a chance that never came, I yanked that motherfucker by the reins.
Didn't wait to be called, I laced up my kicks and put myself in the game.
Little did they know there's a killer instinct I contain.
I took my shot, now these motherfuckers know I ain't playin'.

Don't compare me to a lion when I have the heart of a giant.
Yeah, I was ignored back then, but I've never stayed silent.
I know to some it's tiring, difference is I was built for fighting.
Had a choice, I chose my legacy when most resorted to crying.

Yes, I am going to toot my horn, honk honk motherfucker!

Proud of Myself

I've had moments of triumph after overcoming the failures.
I've seen where most gave up - to forfeit is not in my nature.
Consider it my integrity - the harder the test, the stronger I get to be.
Prior to my salvation, I now see Yeshua meticulously preparing me.

From the decisions I won't forsake or yield into discussions,
To the unforeseen transformation conceived through repercussions,
My bludgeoned soul wandered into the distance - I returned whole.
Survival is an intuition that won't cease to grow old.

Achieved clarity in my journey, although the route took some bad turns.
Altered the perspective - errors converted to lessons learned.

I do what I do because I am who I am regardless of attention or not.

Integrity

Some live for recognition, serving purpose through validation.
Shit, what I look like caring about another nigga's observation?
The sacrifices I've displayed - you think I was served appreciation?
I've heard it verbally, but do the words carry correlation?

I've been dragged through the mud, no excuses, still I get up.
Not concerned if you'd do it for me - I do it just because.
See, if it's about the return, then it never came from the heart.
That's not how I operate - never has been since the start.

Not gon' bullshit - there's an ache that formulates internally.
Sometimes it'd be nice knowing someone would be there for me.
However, I refuse to lower myself and operate in that reliance.
That's why I pride myself on making the most noise in silence.

I'll get my acknowledgement, but not until after my demise.
Not my death - taking responsibility will be the reason for their cries.
Yes, many times I've helped only for them to get the best of me.
As I get left behind, with nothing to show besides my integrity.

Hand on the bible and I swear to tell the truth, the whole truth, and nothing but the truth so help me God!

My Declaration

This be my declaration, something for you to know about my past.
I've always eaten the hell outta pussy, but I ain't never kissed no ass.
What? Is that too vulgar? I got plenty more for you to shoulder.
I always speak my truth, doesn't matter if I am or not sober....

I always speak my truth...
Doesn't matter....
If I am.....
Or not sober......

If you ever met me, you know exactly who I am.
Not a celebrity, just another nigga smoking up a gram.
That hates the society that made me into a man.
What I hadn't yet realized...is what I now understand.

I don't know if it's a calling or some new shit I move with.
Pushing out these manuscripts like I still move bricks.
If I'm a cocky son of a bitch, why is yo bitch on my cock?
Love you, but she'll be leaking me out...whether you like it or not.

I am me because all I can be is this man you see.
A product of the streets eyeing for a seat perched as thee elite.
I'm a commodity...or did I mean oddity? A mixture of both, probably.
Not Socrates with philosophies, pero eso brutál Puerto Rican honesty.

INTERLUDE Single Mothers

Single Mother Appreciation

Nobody asked to take this journey alone, but still that does not stop you.
The responsibility still falls on you for those kids, even if nobody got you.
The ratio of fairness tilts so far against you, still you stay balanced.
It is done so naturally, nobody notices and it sucks that happens.

I see you and the struggles you face, even if you don't understand it.
This is universal, it does not matter if you're White, Black, or Hispanic.
Sons, daughters, if your mom is still alive, do me a favor and call her.
If she is near, please go hug her and then remind her you love her.

After late-night shifts, still came and got us ready for school.
Homework, kissing boo-boos, and assuring our bellies are full.
unconditional sacrifices that go unnoticed to protect our safety.
I saw a mother cry and I asked why, she replied my child actually thanked me.

To all the mothers single-handedly taking care of what they brought to earth.
I thank you from all of us kids who recognize you and value your worth.

ARCH VIII — DUTY

Hey, who got my lighter? How I'm supposed to light this shit? Oh, a match, fuck it.

As the Blunt Burns

The world turns as the blunt continuously burns.
Trying to stay optimistic while life piles up concerns.
There's a rope tied to my waist, dragging me - they're called tasks.
All these responsibilities to manage, I'm wearing too many hats.

No one to help me - or it comes with expectations, so I don't ask.
Feeling used up and then left to dry, sorta like this ash.
How can I be your crutch when I can't even hold my own balance?
I'm not heartless - constant emotional friction got my heart callused.

Doing the best I can with what I got - that's my only available option.
Ironic, this is the richest country and still so many relate to this problem.
The blunt is over, roach in the tray, still I get up and move forward.
Funny thing is, I'm not sure I even know what I'm heading toward.

From a sinner to a winner, how do you like them apples?

Always Equals 7

Yes, I am a winner.

Despite my inadequacies, and I'm a sinner,

Never said I was flawless - just triumphant.

I arrived at each destination I didn't run from.

Put God first, thanked Him for each accomplishment.

Been quite the journey - the trail was especially turbulent.

However, prosperity is not obtained through simplicity.

Diligence, furtherance, and humbleness prior to victory.

Appreciative that the agony of failure didn't go unexperienced.

It formulated my character while building resilience.

Achieved gratification for conquering the process.

Yes, I'm a winner - even when you calculate all the losses.

Alright young bloods, let unc have a talk with ya real quick.

Game for a YN

Hey lil homies running through the world like—
can I holla at you for a sec and tell you what the world like.
Your best friend - that's supposed to be your girl, bro.
Problem is, we weren't brought up to see her as invaluable.

You can be loyal to your homies but their destiny is to be your enemy.
I'm telling you, treat her better than you treat that bottle of Hennessy.
Look bruh, guns are cool - I ain't gon' lie right now I got my strap.
Just don't be fooled, others too can take your ass off the map.

It should never come out of pocket unless it's used with intention.
We gotta learn to resolve conflict in better ways - that's progression.
We are our worst oppressors when we let stereotypes become truth.
We're better than how they address us - now look up like we staring at the roof.

Envision that person you believe is to be respected - then become it.
You're gonna fuck up, and that's ok - but the point is - learn from it.
Now I gave you some game, but you on your own with how you apply it.
Will it be food for thought, or you gon' treat this like you on a diet?

That was some Dr. Seuss bullshit, but the point came clearly across.
Don't ever give up, but know when it's time to walk away from a loss.

Alright, let me take a sec to honor the motherland. Viva Puerto Rico!!

Mi Patria

The blood of my ancestors flows vigorously through my veins.
Inside of my dreams are the echoes of their muffled screams.
Scars inflicted from pain remain, embedded as a permanent stain.
Regardless, we rise to the top, knowing nothing will ever change.

Do I go against the grain? Nope – I create my own lane.
A passionate Taino, I challenge anyone without shame.
Resilience and creativity woven deeply into my African frame.
That natural ability to be an asshole? Comes courtesy of Spain.

Just imagine being chained while told this is the land of the free.
That built a drive in my soul, now I take what is not given to me.
It's not anger, it's authority you hear in my voice when I speak.
I lead my own path, I refuse to walk one that's bleak.

Whether from the island or alla fuera, doesn't matter, this is home.
A home to the most incredible sights the world has ever known.
The music with rhythms that your body can't help but dance.
I'm proud to come from what was never given a chance.

This is for my princess, aka, my heart.

My Heart

The joyous adoration whenever I'm in your presence.
A smile that illuminates the darkest chamber with your essence.
No matter how rugged humanity made me, with you I am soft.
I will serve as your sanctuary up till the instant I am called off.

It's an authority bestowed by God that I will not grasp lightly.
All the brilliance I possess captured in you - anomalously, despite me
The expression to detail my affection for you cannot be illustrated.
For it was the juncture I became your dad - my heart was rehabilitated.

This is for my young king, aka, my legacy.

My Legacy

There comes a time when a man passes down his vision.
The ideologies constructed in the midst of contrition.
The "had I been able to revise shit, this is what I'd do different."
It's a lot, but I want you to surpass me, not be my equivalent.

I've been consistently proud; I just can't let you be complacent.
You've superseded me at your age, and I'm elated to say it.
Hopefully, when you reflect on those scary moments,
Know it was me building you into a champion, not the opponent.

No one was giving the playbook on parenting. Neither did I, nor an example. So I made my own.

Fatherhood

It became this natural instinct, how could it not when you realize the innocence,
from this child I helped bring forth to join adventures within the wilderness.
All I was given was a rock and told to go and figure it out,
so this is my blueprint, with what I had, to just crimper it out.

Nervousness rises as my breathing increases, this one I cannot fail.
I've fucked up so much, but this is non-optional, I must prevail.
Diaper changes, dodged a stream, still got shit on my fingernail.
Like that even matters, for my two seeds I'll stand up to the devil in hell.

A few important lessons: know when to act, but fear no man.
Don't trust people that are always in need of a friend.
Life's a bitch, but at the end of the day, you control your emotions.
Take accountability, but not the blame. Never lie, and sharks are in every ocean.

The negligence of my kin will not become my definition.
The cycle stops with me being the final repetition.
The only pain seen is through the uncontrolled tears from my eyes.
After I wipe them dry, the vision's clear: they're the reason God wants me
alive.

Paying homage: Rose That Grew from Concrete
2025

<u>Rose That Grew from Concrete 2025</u>

Fell along the cracks, still rooted to plant.
Found a source to grow where nothing else can.
unbelievable - a silent achievement.
But no one will believe you - no one will see it.

It runs its course in silence - a rose unseen.
Till it withers its last petal, crushed on the street.
If you're wondering - what does this all mean?
The impossible can happen - don't get stuck in your dreams!

ARCH IX — LETTERS

To all my homies, good or bad. This for y'all!

<u>Strictly 4 My Niggaz</u>

To all my homies that shared some time with me in this thing called life.
Even the ones I don't talk to, whether I did or didn't do right.
Proud of us that found hope amongst the hopeless.
Achieved our goals, leaving dead weight behind- remaining focused.

It's all love on this side as I cheer for all of your successes.
Fuck all the bullshit, looking back now, we was all reckless.
Especially me, I ain't gon' front, I know I could be extra.
If I'm honest, it was fear mixed with unbearable pressure.

A few stuck around and now we get to enjoy our own family.
Barbecues, birthdays, and bloodcurdling stories recalled happily.
Labeled a crazed bunch, really our environment made us honest.
We're many things but never ignorant in getting goals accomplished.

I put one in the air for all of my niggaz whose souls disappeared.
Destiny could only allow so much - the odds were never meant to be fair.
Gazing above the clouds, arms stretched asking the Almighty in heaven.
May you bring peace in abundance to each and every one of my brethren.

Cherry, you already know.

<u>Cherry</u>

Cherry, what can I say in 16 bars about you and me?
I cherished our time together - that's undoubtedly.
Scared of being hurt, so you asked me to find someone else.
I didn't care - I wanted you, even risking your mental health.

You opened up - yup, and so did I.
We were both guarded but saw no reason why.
What we shared is real - that's something no one can take from us.
When you think of me - hopefully smilin', with no hate for us.

Never said it before - knowing you don't believe anymore - but I love you.
There might be distance, sure - but I'm lying if I said I don't think of you.
Actually, I pray for you every day - I pray for your kids too.
Guess the timing was off - guess we doing what we gots to do.

You deserve to be happy, Cherry - you deserve your peace.
Don't worry about me - I can be found, keep your mind at ease.
Despite your beliefs, you were never a rebound or part of some pattern.
Everything I spoke was 100 - can't speak for others, but to me you matter.

Our story ends where we remain apart - no fairytale reunion.
I'll always be just a call away, no matter what I'm doing.

Primo en el cielo, miss you cuz!

Tito

Primo, I feel sorrow when I think about you - yet I smile.
So many golden moments - but none will be new now.
There ain't shit we can change - it's sealed in time, literally.
I've made my peace with you - and pray you've forgiven me.

We were shaped by the streets, born of our environment.
But you diverged - chose a path different than I went.
Our bond once felt unbreakable - then I had to walk away.
One of the hardest truths I lived was leaving you astray.

You wept, "How could you do this?" - but you broke my heart.
Time and again, you unraveled - choosing to fall apart.
It's a weight I still bear - letting go was never easy.
But I never stopped loving you - and I hope you believe me.

I'm not without fault, cuz - I'm fucked up too.
I ruin everything I ever said I love you to.
I just had to release this - had to get it off my chest.
Man, we had some wild nights - some of the absolute best.

How many times did we sneak out, snatching your dad's rum?
Acting reckless - how dafuq could they not know we were drunk?
We had weed but no papers - so once we used a receipt,
Worst mistake ever - ended with a headache and vomit on the street.

I'll never forget the night we killed that fifth of 151.
You were about to be a dad, and I was becoming an unc.
That's why I still smile - even when your memory makes me sad.
I love you, primo - thank you for some of the best times I ever had.

Big bro, I ain't forget about you my nigga!

I Am My Brother's Keeper

We two peas from different pods that fell along the same tree.
We weren't supposed to be, but destiny turned us into family.
Tragically, a turn was taken that totally switched up our reality.
You was both a witness to and a participant in my tragedies.

Two bastards taken in, sharing life, fighting over every meal.
When we was little, we'd go snuff for snuff, even when our skin peeled.
Obviously we healed, Mamita didn't - you know how that made us both feel.
After her, we didn't depend on nobody, we got us - a bond forged in steel.

It didn't always remain forged, but that's not something we gon talk about.
I talked enough about then, Big Bro - let me talk in regard to now.
We both miss Tito, we was a trinity, now it's back to us two.
We had our odds, and our ends, but forever you know I love you.

It's kinda cool taking a sip - watching our kids jump on the trampoline.
We're misfitted, but we fit together, kind of like fire and gasoline.
It doesn't need to be said, but if one of us is dead, the kids will be fed.
For now, cheers to the many years as we look forward to what lies ahead.

Mis hijos, thought I just wrote one for you guys, c'mon now. Haha.

Marcos and Mia

To my pride and to my joy, the two spirits that define my existence.
I know you know dad is different, but my love for you holds no resistance.
I try hard to hide my internal scars, I'm sorry when I fall short.
It is never your fault, and I'd rather suffer than see you two hurt.

Never worry for me, that's not your burden, it's mine to withstand.
All I ask is that you always give it your all, stay true to our brand.
Yes, I am strict because I know what I had to reap before I could sow.
I'll never shelter you from a deceitful world, that'll stunt your growth.

Marcos, when I initially held you, that was the first time I ever felt whole.
We looked into each other's eyes and I swear, I never wanted to let go.
Please don't ever mistake my toughness for anything but my belief in you.
My prayer, Papito, is one day you'll see the greatness...that I see in you.

Mia, what a chaotic entrance, yet you slept calmly on my bare chest.
I assume that's the moment I became a king, since you're my princess.
Hope you understand I can't always be gentle, I need you to be strong.
My prayer, Baby, is that you keep going for every fucking thing you want.

You two are my heart and also you two are my legacy.
I wish I could fully articulate what you two have meant to me.
No crying at my funeral, I need you two to show strength for me.
An endearing asshole, that's how I hope you two...will remember me.

Of all the shitty things I did in life, this is my worst moment.

To my unborn child

I tried to write this with a sober mind and tearless eyes.
But I can't, so I'ma sip a bottle of Fireball as my emotions rise.
See, your conception was the result of a pleasant surprise.
Thought I was safe with a vasectomy, nothing but lies.

Nevertheless, the responsibility was mine and I took it with pride.
Getting out of bed, changing your diaper, then singing you a lullaby.
Seeking you throughout the house as your silly self would hide.
Drying your face free of moisture from every tear you cried.

Picturing you getting taller, feeling brave, and becoming a challenge.
That makes me laugh because it's hard to get your dad off balance.
I know you would've been a combination of witty and bold.
I would have clocked that before you turned any years old.

Watching you walk across the stage, grabbing a diploma in your hands.
Sending you off to be your own, letting you choose where you land.
Then you bring home a partner, someone you may marry.
Asking for advice because sometimes life gets scary.

I'm not going to talk about anyone else - this is between you and I.
I did everything I could, I swear, I never wanted you to die.
I know you're in heaven if there's a spot for me, keep it in reserve.
I can't be mad if I go to hell, honestly, it's what I deserve.

One last stop on the healing train before I reach my destination. Say hello to lil me.

Letter to Me

Hey there lil' nigga, what's goin on wit'cha?
Take a seat, let present day me talk to ya.
You see it's common for a genius to talk to thyself.
So I'ma do that as we take a walk with myself.

First off, on the reals we gotta give mom a break.
She'd have never chosen the inevitable to be our fate.
What those men did to us behind closed doors was not our fault.
Yea, they never got caught - but they still gotta face God, real talk.

Remember when we tried to holla at hoes and they zoned us as friends?
Now these bitches come to us, all we had to do was gain inner confidence.
Streets gave us so many adventures, most importantly they taught us who we weren't.
It was hard because where we from it's dangerous to swim against the current.

If there is one thing the pain, betrayal, and heartache gave us, it's courage.
The hurt almost broke us, we still pulled through, so be proud we earned it!
Those nights wishing we was aborted and would never appear.
Look at Marcos and Mia, now tell me we shouldn't be here.

I can't say we figured it all out and now life is all peachy.
But I can say we defied our odds, you best believe me.
Appreciate all the turmoil you endured when we was a kid.
Now I need you to rest - I'll take it from here, trust me, I got this!

Mom, we close this book with you, One last conflict to overcome...

Letter to Mom Monologue

To close, not only this chapter, but to conclude the book in itself. I have written my most vulnerable piece - a letter to my mother who passed in 1989. I was born in 1982, so I didn't get much time with her.

A normal question or statement I get is do you know if she's proud of you. So to my mother I say this:

Mom, I know you've seen me do unforgivable things. Things I'll have to answer when the day comes and I have to look God in his eyes. You've seen me at the lowest of my personal humanity. I'm sorry to have to make you see your only child become such a person.

But as you've also witnessed, I didn't allow my fall to be my fate. I opened my eyes, picked my head up, put ten down, moved forward, and never looked back.

I know you're proud of me and the man I became, the father I am still becoming, and the man of God I am destined by him to be.

I love you mom, and I'm sorry for the moments of anger I have held towards you. I know it's not your fault, I know it's not what you would have chosen for me.

And Mom, you need to know - I forgive you.

<u>Mom</u>

Bendición momma, it's ya baby boy - how's it been?
Hold up, give me a sec (hiccup) I'ma swallow this hen.
Fuck pops - but why you passed when I was six?
I love you, mom - but you didn't give me shit.

Well... you gave me life.
That quickly turned into strife.
Not your fault - who woulda knew.
I'm sure you sorrowed, witnessing what I went through.

Not sure what was worse - the beatings or the molestations.
I learned not to feel pain - it's how I survived those occasions.
They took advantage since I had no one to run to.
Incorporated a mentality - from kind to fuck you.

Confused, refused, excluded - often to be forgotten.
My perception for life had no purpose - my soul must be rotten.
Encountered peace through green leaves and beverages that burn.
12 stop to shove my face in the ground, sayin', "Boy, you gon learn."

Irritated they found nothing in my possession.
Momma, I'm no fool - you saw I had secret locations.
I apologize for the violence I caused.
No excuses, mom - however, I was lost.

shit, I can't even conclude I've yet to be found.
As I strive to maintain a foundation that's mentally sound.
Seen your grandkids? They're so incredible.
Mom - it's eerie how much Mia resembles you.

Our wit, I showed her grit - the beauty's already in her.
Marcos got our flex, in the chest - developing charisma.
Best thing, momma - they never experienced what I did.
My greatest achievement - never shall I wish the opposite.

Am I perfect? Mom, you know I'm far from it.
It was worth it, Mom - it's ok I'm being honest.
You are in me, as I am of your flesh
I'm good, mom - meet you at my death

I love you, Mom. R.I.P.

Prayer

Dear Lord,
Thank you for this gift,
Thank you for this ability.
Most importantly,
Thank you for forgiving me.

Outro

Man, this was fun. Thank you.
If you made it this far, I appreciate you.
Most importantly, thank you for your time—
not necessarily your money.
You might've pirated this book,
or you're reading a friend's copy...
Either way, thank you for giving me your time.
I hope you enjoyed my storytelling,
My rhyme patterns,
My variations,
and my truth.
This was my healing journey,
Some names and situations changed
We have to protect the innocent, or guilty...
I know I'm unique —
but somehow I feel completely normal.
Isn't that crazy?